The WARLORD'S BEADS

The WARLORD'S BEADS

Virginia Walton Pilegard

Illustrated by
Nicolas Debon

PELICAN PUBLISHING COMPANY
Gretna 2001

To Richard, Neil, Timothy, William,
and all who count—VWP
To my parents—ND

The word "Pelican" and the depiction of a
pelican are trademarks of Pelican Publishing Company, Inc., and are
registered in the U.S. Patent and Trademark Office.

Library of Congress Cataloging-in-Publication Data
Pilegard, Virginia Walton.
    The warlord's beads / written by Virginia Walton Pilegard ; illustrated by Nicolas Debon.
        p. cm.
    Summary: A young Chinese boy helps his father count the warlord's vast treasures by using beads
threaded on a branch. Includes a brief history of the abacus and instructions for making one.
    ISBN 1-56554-863-9
    [1. Abacus—Fiction. 2. Counting—Fiction. 3. China—Fiction.] I. Debon, Nicolas, ill. II. Title.

PZ7.P6283 Wap 2001
[E]—dc21

00-049125

Printed in Hong Kong
Published by Pelican Publishing Company, Inc.
1000 Burmaster Street, Gretna, Louisiana 70053

THE WARLORD'S BEADS

Many years ago in China a boy named Chuan lived with his father in the palace of a powerful warlord. One day he realized his father was worried.

How could that be? The sky was bright with sunlight. A songbird sat on the curve of the swooping roof of the warlord's palace. Chuan picked a soft, ripe peach from a tree in the palace garden. When he took a bite, sweet juice ran down his chin.

Since they had come to live with the warlord, he and Father always had enough to eat. The warlord trusted only Father to sort and count his treasures. Maybe Father was lonely working all alone.

When the warlord's three sons found Chuan wandering around the palace they chased him with switches made from slender peach branches. Today, he decided, he must be brave. He crept through the palace. At last he reached the door of the counting room.

ather's eyes were squeezed shut. The corners of his mouth turned down. Around him elegant carved boxes overflowed with bead necklaces. Bronze coins, spices, and incense spilled out of leather bags. Jade statues of many sizes glowed white and pink and green.

Chuan slipped over to his father and touched the sleeve of his robe. Father's eyes opened wide with surprise. "Every time he rides away, the warlord brings back more for me to count," he muttered.

"**I** am only a poor peasant. It is too much."

"Honorable Father," Chuan said, "the warlord gave you this job because he knows you are clever."

"The warlord says I am so clever that I have found a way to steal from him." Chuan could not believe what his father was saying.

esterday I counted one hundred twenty carved boxes. The day before I counted one hundred twenty-nine. Yesterday I counted one hundred sixty-seven bags of incense. The day before, one hundred seventy-one. More came from the last journey and I have counted less!" Father dropped his face into his hands.

"When I begin to count, a servant comes and I lose my place. The warlord's sons run through like wild animals and I must start again."

"Could I help?" Chuan asked.

Father thought. "You could hold up one finger each time I count ten boxes. That would help me remember what I have counted." Chuan nodded eagerly.

father touched the precious boxes one by one, placing them into piles of ten. Chuan held up fingers first on one hand, then on the other.

"Eighty, ninety, one hundred boxes." And still there were more. Chuan looked at his outstretched fingers and wondered what to do next. "Father, I have used all ten fingers."

"Take off your shoes," Father said. "Each toe can stand for one hundred. Then you can use your fingers to count more piles of ten." Chuan pulled off his shoes. He held up a toe. Now he had fingers enough to count more, but it was not going to be easy holding up one toe at a time. One hundred ten—one toe and one finger.

A servant came with a tray of sweetmeats. "Count well, peasant, or we will all be punished for your stupidity," he growled. Father did not look up. Chuan was afraid even to wiggle his toe.

The servant left. Father ignored the tray. He looked at the one toe and one finger Chuan held in the air. He looked at the five boxes in the pile he had just started and nodded with satisfaction. "One hundred fifteen." He began to count again.

Chuan could almost taste the sweets. He wished the tray were closer. He thought about stretching his tongue.

J ust then, in ran the warlord's three
sons. Chuan ducked his head waiting
for them to swat him with their switches.

They ran toward him, but the oldest noticed the tray of sweets. They dropped their switches, took handfuls of sweets, and then ran out of the room.

"What was the last number?" Father asked. Chuan looked at his hands and feet. He had lost track when the boys ran at him.

father sighed and started over. Chuan wished Father had scolded him. He picked up one of the hateful switches the warlord's sons had dropped and threaded a large jade bead onto it.

An idea began to form in his mind. If he put ten beads on each switch, he could move one to the top each time father called out a number. It would be better than fingers and toes. Excited, he began to push beads onto the other two switches.

A servant girl came in with a pot of tea and a delicious-smelling dish of roasted duck and rice. "The warlord will be home tomorrow," she stammered. She almost spilled the tea. "If we stop to eat, we will lose count," Father said in a weary voice.

"I know a way that we could stop," Chuan said.

Before Father could say no, Chuan pointed to the three switches lying on the floor. Each switch had ten beads. On the first switch, one bead was pushed all the way to the top. On the second switch, three beads were at the top. On the third switch, one bead was at the top.

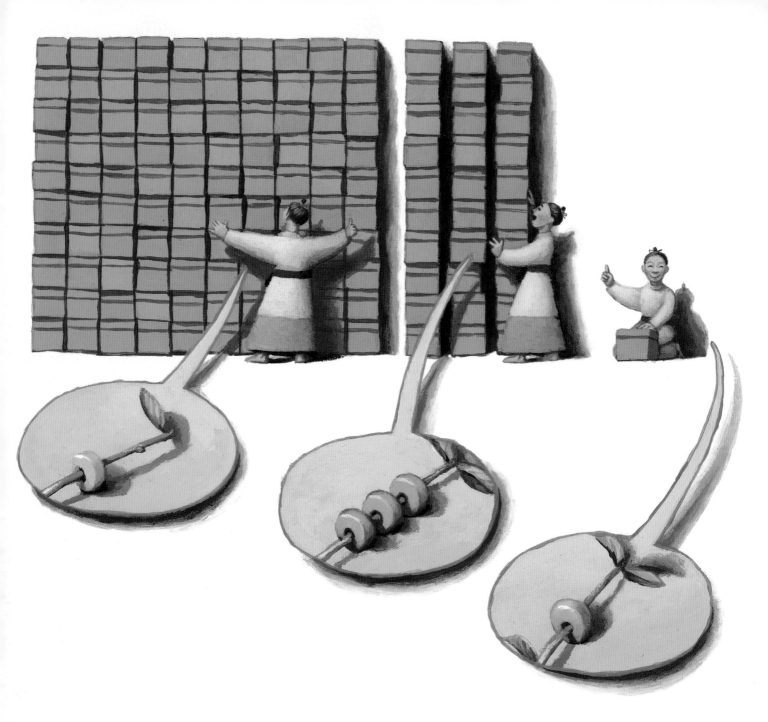

"The first switch tells us we have one pile of one hundred carved boxes, the second one says we have three piles of ten, and the third one says we have a pile with just one box."

father smiled. "One hundred thirty-one," he said and stopped to eat the roasted duck and rice.

By nightfall, Father and Chuan finished counting all of the warlord's treasures. They found more carved boxes, jade statues, and bags of spices, coins, and incense than Father had ever counted before.

he next morning, they counted
again just for good measure. When
the warlord returned, he was so pleased he
told Father to keep all the precious beads
that Chuan had used on his counting sticks.
"Peasant," the warlord announced, "I will
see that your son becomes apprentice to
a fine teacher. Someday he will be an
important man in China."

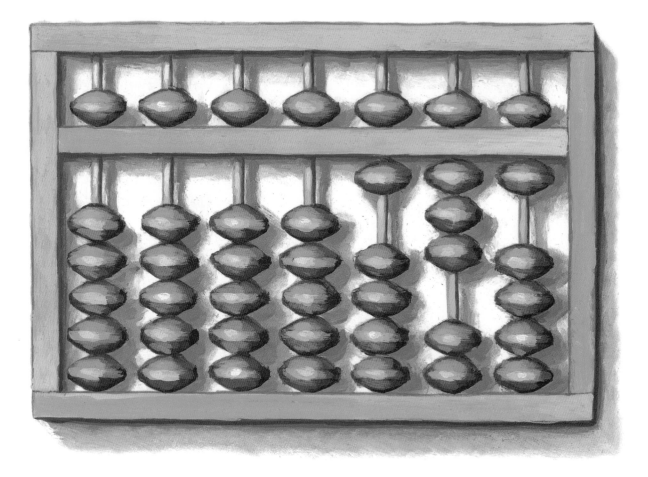

You may have guessed that Chuan used beads and switches to make a counting frame—a forerunner of the abacus. Writings from China's Tang dynasty, A.D. 618 to 906, tell of several kinds of counting frames. By the fourteenth century, the abacus became the favorite "calculator" throughout Asia, where it is still used by some shopkeepers.

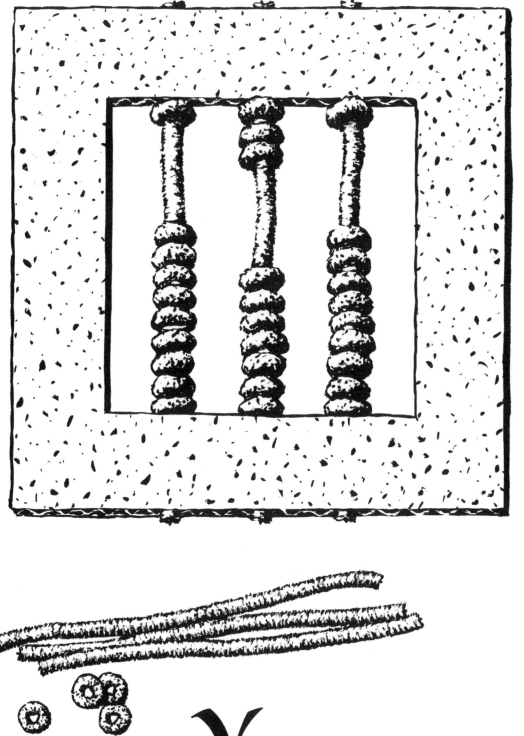

Y ou can make your own counting beads. Just take Fruit Loops or other colored cereal that is in the shape of *O*s and thread onto pipe cleaners. A cardboard frame may be traced from this page.